I Am a Kid-trepreneur

A Guideline for Kids by a Kid

A Recipe for a Successful Kid Business

by

Delphine Nephtalie Dauphin

RoseDog Books
PITTSBURGH, PENNSYLVANIA 15238

The contents of this work, including, but not limited to, the accuracy of events, people, and places depicted; opinions expressed; permission to use previously published materials included; and any advice given or actions advocated are solely the responsibility of the author, who assumes all liability for said work and indemnifies the publisher against any claims stemming from publication of the work.

All Rights Reserved
Copyright © 2017 by Delphine Nephtalie Dauphin

No part of this book may be reproduced or transmitted, downloaded, distributed, reverse engineered, or stored in or introduced into any information storage and retrieval system, in any form or by any means, including photocopying and recording, whether electronic or mechanical, now known or hereinafter invented without permission in writing from the publisher.

RoseDog Books
585 Alpha Drive
Pittsburgh, PA 15238
Visit our website at *www.rosedogbookstore.com*

ISBN: 978-1-4809-7705-1
eISBN: 978-1-4809-7684-9

DEDICATION

I dedicate this book to my mother, Nephtalie Hyacinthe, for allowing me start my own business. She let me be Boss Girl. She has thought me the value of discipline, education, confidence, and money. She is constantly training me to be a great person in society, and I love it. You are a great mommy!

I want to thank my whole family:

My papa and manman, Reverend and Mrs. Prosper Hyacinthe for spoiling me; and My Uncle, Reverend John Hyacinthe and his wife Genita, for cheering me on always. Uncle, thanks for being my very first customer. I want to thank my wonderful tickle buddy, Auntie Benghie Hyacinthe for treating me like her own and for helping with the management of my business. You are a force in my life. Thanks to Uncle John B.; Auntie Vasthie; Uncle Ronel; my father, Harold Dauphin; and my brother, Harold Matthew. Gigie you are amazeballs. Disha, you always show up whenever I need you for my business, you are more like a sister. Jahmahr, you would do anything to help me promote my business and I love the jingle that you created.

Thanks to my Extended family: Nancy Baptiste, for sharing the love of baking with me; and Kayla and Eliette, for your time and your support. Cassandre, I thank you for offering help, even when your time is restricted, and my Great Aunt Jislaine.

Thank you to my Mentors:

Ms. Sonia Chess, you have been teaching me etiquette and poise since the age of four, and now being an ambassador at your organization is such a blessing.

Ms. Ernisha Randolph your marketing skill is unbelievable. You take the time to sit with me and make sure that my ideas matter. I know you will take me far.

Mrs. Lorraine Sims-Kirkland, you continue to share your talent with me, helping me create new recipes, allowing me to be wild and to have fun while baking.

Besties: Jaylan (my cousin by choice), Autumn, Aniya, Amaya, Olivia, and Kaliyah you are my greatest helpers. I love you guys.

Friends of the family: Ms. April Jones, Mrs. Erica Johnson, and Ms. Elisha Fuentes you are all my other mommies in business and in life. Hugs and kisses. Myrtho Jean-Baptiste, Thank you for being part of my team.

Thank you to my school for believing in me and supporting me, Go Titans! My church, Sheridan Hills (My Awana team), thank you again to all of you.

I want to thank God for everything, because I know he is the master of possibilities.

"I don't want a doll. I want to create one."

At the age of four all, I wanted was to start my own business. I didn't understand what a business was, but I wanted to create things and sell them. I was good at collecting money for my school fundraisers. I felt like I could do anything. I kept asking my mommy if I could start my own business, because I had been baking since I could walk. I learned about money very early. I always had a budget, and I believed in giving my 10 percent to the church.

One day I begged my mommy to allow me to start my own business. I was sure it was going to be a cupcake business. So, I did some research on what was needed to have a baking business. Yes, there is a lot of help available online, in the community or just by talking to grownups. Here is the recipe that can help you become a great Kid-trepreneur.

Step #1
"You must want to do it, not Mommy or Daddy."

The parents should never force the child to start a business. You have to want to be an entrepreneur. Do not do it because your friend is selling cupcakes. You have to want it. I love to bake and have been doing it for a longtime. I knew that I could do it. In fact, I knew I could do it well. I knew that I could bake cupcakes that others would enjoy. I wanted my own business because I did not want a traditional job. I have always done things at home. Once I knew my colors, I separated the clothes on laundry day. If you try your best and your parents are watching, they will see that you want to do things on your own. You have to prove yourself. It has to be what you want.

Do you want to have your own business? _____
_____
_____
_____
_____

Why do you want it? _____
_____
_____
_____
_____

Motivation:

I can do ALL things...

Step #2
"Practice, practice, practice."

Now that you know you want a business, you have to practice a lot. It's not a fairy tale. It's not *alakazam, alakazoom*. It is hard work. You have to make sure you take care of your school work first, then schedule a time for your business. My business hours start Friday evening and end on Sunday afternoon.

What time can you put aside for your business? If you are very young, you will definitely need the help of your parents. Make sure the time works for everyone involved. In my cupcake business, I am too young to turn on the oven, so I have an adult or teenager do it for me. Always make sure the schedule works for everyone.

I practice a lot. I practice with older people who have been baking longer than I have. I ask my customers for ideas. I go to the local bakeries and ask questions.

You will be surprised how many people are willing to help. You just have to ask. I go to the park like every kid, I have good grades, I have play dates, I play music, I dance ballet, and I bake. I give myself three to four hours for work. I also use some of my business money to take classes on cupcake decorations and I attend cake expos, so I can meet people that share the same interests as me.

How do you plan to get better at working on your business? _____
_____
_____
_____
_____

What days will you be open for business? _____
_____
_____
_____
_____

How many hours will you work on your business? _____
_____
_____
_____
_____

Where can you learn more? _____
_____
_____
_____
_____

Who can teach you more? _____
_____
_____
_____
_____

Motivation:

I practice, therefore my perfect practice will make perfect

Step #3
"Do what brings you joy. Do what you like."

Invent something you enjoy. If you don't like lemonade, please do not have a lemonade business. Do what you have talent for. Go where your heart guides you. You have to be good at it. I mentioned I have been baking since I could walk. It was a bonding time for my mommy and me. She does not really like to bake, but she wanted me to learn a few things in the kitchen. My mommy can bake, but she does not enjoy it unless it's a bonding moment. She loves to cook and I can see it in her eyes. I play the piano, but I am not crazy for it. Ballet is my passion; I do a ballet move every chance I get. It is the same for baking. You can see the twinkle in my eyes when I bake. I also love my products. I am my own customer. I believe that if you like it a whole lot, you will make it work. If you can't make it work on your own, ask for help. Get someone to manage the business for you, while you still have the final say.

What brings you joy? _____
_____
_____
_____
_____

Do your eyes twinkle thinking about it? _____
_____
_____
_____
_____

Can you manage it by yourself? _____
_____
_____
_____
_____

Dream about your business like you are in the future...What do you see? Describe it. _____
_____
_____
_____
_____

Motivation:

My skill will stand before all.

Step #4
"Compete, but don't copy."

Competition is good. I like competition because it helps me do better. It's like a challenge. You can't go to your local store and copy what they do. What they do should bring a better idea to your business. Would you watch television, if every program was the same? Wouldn't you get tired, if every lemonade tasted the same?

Competition helps me get creative. I love to run with my closest cousin, Ron. He is an athlete, a future pro-soccer player. When we race, I can see him slow down when he does not sense me behind him. The fact that we are in a competition makes him run faster. The faster I run, the faster he gets. At the end of the day, both of us exercise and we are both happy. That's how I compete. I compete with others who are better than me. I compete with people I can learn from. I don't want to be my cousin Ron. He will be a professional soccer player one day. I don't want to do what he does. I want to be Delphine.

Copying is really bad, even if you only do it once. No one will trust your ideas and everyone will doubt everything you do.

Who is your competition? _____
_____
_____
_____
_____

What is it that you like about that person business? _____
_____
_____
_____
_____

Motivation:

I will win the race...

Step #5
"Protect your business."

Make sure you only share with friends you trust. It can't be someone you just met. The friendship has to be long enough. I trusted my friends Autumn and Aniya, because we have been friends since Pre-K. I know they want the best for me. I know they will not do anything to hurt me. They are my real BFF's. They come and they help me with my business. I am fine with them seeing what I do at work.

If you have recipes like I do, protect them. You can protect them by putting them in a safe. You can protect them by putting a password on your tablet. Just because you do not copy, it does not mean that someone else won't. You don't want someone else to steal your business that you have worked very hard for.

Do you have recipes, formulas or how-to's? _____
_____
_____
_____
_____

How will you protect them? _____
_____
_____
_____
_____

How much will it cost to protect your business? _____
_____
_____
_____
_____

Motivation:

I will be careful with my business.

Step #6
"Give, help, and give again"

In my church, we give coins to help the children's ministry. The more we give, the more activities we get. The more we give, more snacks were given to us. I told you before that my eyes twinkle when I hear math, so I understand that easily. I give my 10 percent—use a calculator if you have to—and I receive way more, because they put all the kids' money together. I give 10 percent, because that's what I believe in. I see it in the Bible and it works. I was at an expo and a little girl wanted a cupcake, but it seemed like her mommy didn't have enough money. I gave her one and I paid for it myself. She was so happy and I was happier.

I paid for it because I pay myself first. I have my own pocket money and I don't mix it with the profit of my business. Don't go in your business and start giving money away. You have to be disciplined. Give from what you have. Don't give away your business.

Who needs your help? _____
_____
_____
_____
_____

What percentage will you give yourself? _____
_____
_____
_____
_____

How much can you give to others with a happy heart, knowing that you will not get it back? _____
_____
_____
_____
_____

Motivation:
I will help the least of these…

Step #7
"Sell. Sell your personality. Sell your product. Sell."

I attended a workshop in which they were talking about kids and money. I knew I wanted a business. I begged my mommy to let me start the business and she was not fond of the idea. I was glad she was there. I don't know what they said in her class, she came out saying, "Okay, you can start your business, but only on weekends." I was excited. All I wanted was one day and now I had a weekend! Thank you, Jesus! Mommy also mentioned that if I got one "B" in school, the business will be closed. On our way home, I had to sell myself. I told my mom that I would stay on all "A's", I would do chores, I would be on green, and I would go to bed on time. Sell, Sell, Sell.

I called my family, my mom's friends, and my friends parents and announced my new business. I started with my Uncle J.W. (Uncle Baby) and my Aunty Martha Benghie, because they like to cheer me on. I used a pre-mixed cupcake with everything in it that was purchased for me for $5. I wanted to have many clients, so I could only sell each person one cupcake. I was happy to continue making calls because my uncle and my aunt said yes. I called my other Aunt, Aunt Va, I called my grandma, I called my mom's childhood friend Emma, my cousin Disha, and before you knew it, I was sold out. That $5 became $27, because some people tipped me.

I never once had to use extra money from my parents towards the business. I now bake from scratch and create my own recipes. I never forget to offer my products. I sell every weekend. I am very nice to them. If you don't treat your customers nicely, they won't buy from you. My aunt's neighbor is my customer for life because I treat him very nicely and now his kids buy from me too.

Tips:
    a) Create a sales pitch. It can be a few sentences that explain who you are, your business name, your product, your price, and how it will benefit the person.
    b) Sell to people you know will say yes first, so you don't get discouraged.
    c) Hand out your business cards.

d) Exchange numbers.

e) Do not be afraid to offer; it's not about you. They don't reject you; maybe they don't have money now.

f) Sell your personality. You are your business. Smile, be polite, and offer them while you shake your head up and down for "yes."

Motivation:
I am a kid-trepreneur...

Step #8
"Make it legal."

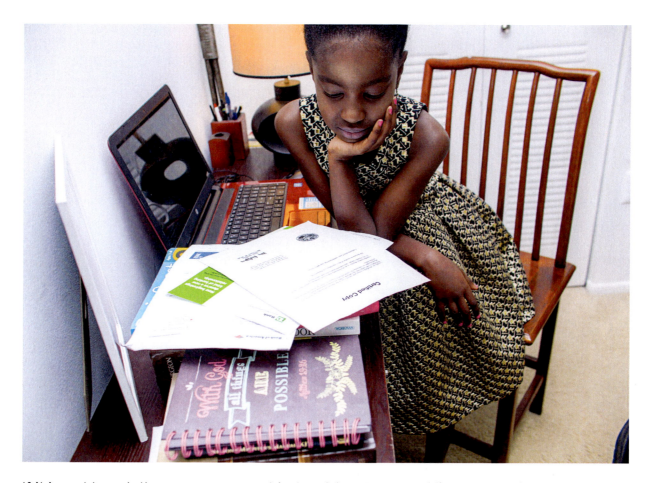

If it is not legal, then you can get in trouble. You need licenses. This is also a way to prove that your business can be trusted. In less than a month, my business became legal. I was starting to get customers in my neighborhood and they were referring other people to me that I don't even know. I don't know how to do these things. I just know how to bake, but I was very involved in the process, so I will share with you.

Meet with a business person, or if you have someone in your family who studied Business use them, it will be cheaper or even free.

Meet with an accountant. Usually they are the same people who help with taxes. There are different guidelines based on how much money you make.

Meet with a lawyer, in order to make sure that you have authority in your business. The lawyer can translate the legal papers into simple English. Use a lawyer when you can afford one.

Meet with your business manager, someone who can help you manage the business better, so you can focus on your talent. In my case, it's my Aunt Benghie.

Marketing, public relations, and advertising consultations will help a great deal. If you can afford it, it's worth it.

I am blessed that I have family members and friends who helped me with these things. Use your connections.

I will give my business power...

Step #9
"Business is fun and serious."

I love my business so much because it brings me joy. If an egg accidentally drops, I laugh it out. At the same time, I make sure that everything is correct. I can't play around when I have a customer in front of me. There is a time and a place for everything. I like to play music when I am baking. It is so much fun.

Do you take your business seriously? _____
_____
_____
_____
_____

Do you play around all the time while you are working? _____
_____
_____
_____
_____

How do you have fun while working on your business? _____
_____
_____
_____
_____

Motivation:

I laugh because it's everything ...

"I am cheering for you!"

While you have some fun, business has to be serious. I started my business because I wanted to have an early start. I want to go to college and let my employees work on the business. I want to invest part of my money, so it can grow faster. I don't like quitters because they complain a lot. Keep trying and never give up. If you lose a customer, try to get them back and keep looking for more. Following these recipes will help your business growth.

Good Luck! I am cheering for you. Whooooohooooooooo!